THE
NEW NORMAL:

Digitization, Digitalization and E-commerce in International Business

BY

LEFOR JOSEPH LEFOR

AuthorHouse™ UK
1663 Liberty Drive
Bloomington, IN 47403 USA
www.authorhouse.co.uk
UK TFN: 0800 0148641 (Toll Free inside the UK)
UK Local: 02036 956322 (+44 20 3695 6322 from outside the UK)

Because of the dynamic nature of the Internet, any web addresses or links contained in this book may have changed since publication and may no longer be valid. The views expressed in this work are solely those of the author and do not necessarily reflect the views of the publisher, and the publisher hereby disclaims any responsibility for them.

Any people depicted in stock imagery provided by Getty Images are models, and such images are being used for illustrative purposes only. Certain stock imagery © Getty Images.

This book is printed on acid-free paper.

ISBN: 978-1-6655-8121-9 (sc)
ISBN: 978-1-6655-8120-2 (e)

Print information available on the last page.

Published by AuthorHouse 10/22/2020

authorHOUSE®

THE NEW NORMAL:

Digitization, Digitalization and E-commerce in International Business

BY

LEFOR JOSEPH LEFOR

(2020)

DEDICATION

❖ To the Lefor's family.

The figure heads hear include:
Mr. Lefor Louis from Balikumbat and **Mrs. Lefor Margaret** from Bafut.

ACKNOWLEDGEMENTS

I count myself the wealthiest person in the world. This has nothing to do with my bank account but everything to do with the countless great minds God destined to cross my path in life.

Let me use this profound opportunity to think of as many significant figures as have been in my life's journey till this day. These include but not limited to: **My heavenly father, my family, friends, teachers, colleagues (including my managers of the various institutions I have been part of).**

Before I start mentioning people, let me acknowledge the **giver of all knowledge**. I serve an **omniscient God.** This book is just one of the billions of wonders he does for me.

Family:

Mum & dad (to whom this book is dedicated), Mrs. Lefor Christiana, Mr. Lefor Divine, Mrs. Lefor Mady, Lefor Dan Andrew, Mrs. Bula Quinta and Petyin Derien.

Friends and teachers:

Arrey Bate, Nke Cynthia, Momo Bertrand, Ufembe Romeo, Herman Yves, Sidonie Fotso, Sharon Nguetna, Silenou Arnauld, Anim Desmond, Anim Carlson, Sunjo Cedric, Simon Tagne, Nyuydine Collins, Ewane Anoch, Kamto Raissa, Mabel Yinyuy, Yong Magdala, Ivana Leba, Ebi Roseline, Afanwi Neba, Kumo Glen, Alami Angele, Ngu Fomede, Hillary Prisca, Awah Erica, Swirri Thelma, Moutchipou Laura, Eku Bernadette, Joy Cee, Ngah Christopher, Mr Paul Vincent, Eposi Frida, Ekorh Shiphrah, Anchi Dorcas, Tse Tsang, Bawum Mercy, Chinedu Jude, Frankie Atanga, Yihan Jiang, Anita Mwuesh, Nsoyuka Stephen and Denroy Anogho.

Mr. Fotachi Michael, Mr. Mbilam Samson, Rev Fr. Jervis, Mme. Dinah Fungeh, Mr. Nji Paul, Mr. Ndah Grimbald, Mr. Tamafor Elvis, Mr. Tanwie Valerie, Mr. Makia Mpok, Mr. Leo Orobor, Dr. Gatchu Harry, Dr. Noah Kofi Karley, Dr. Swetketu Patnaik, Dr. Rob Willis, Dr. Sandra Selmanovic, Mrs. Cheryl Greyson, Dr. Helen Benton, Mr. Chun Tu.

Managers and colleagues:

Mrs. Nicola Faulkner, Mrs. Donna Franklin, Mrs. Margarita, Mrs. Marina Tansley, Mr. Chris Welhams, Mr. Suneet Bakarania, Mr. Nana Adom, Mr. Adrian McDonald, Mrs. Claire Wookey, Mr. Darren Leader, Mrs. Helga Cole, Mr. Ernest, Rio Godfrey, Lindsay Luckins, Joanne Shiret, Becca, Vicky and Adella

Key institutions:

Catholic School Alakuma, Mankon - Bamenda. Key Figure head at the time: Mrs. Angeline Awah.

Sacred Heart College (SAHECO) Douala. Key figure heads at the time: Rev Sister Christine Ndukwe and Sir Athanas Duma.

Presbyterian Secondary School (P.S.S) Mankon. Key figure head at the time: Mr. Kimah Constantine.

Catholic University of Cameroon - CATUC Bamenda. Key figure heads at the time: Rev Fr. Michael Suh Niba and Rev Fr. Joseph Owoh.

Anglia Ruskin University, Cambridge, United Kingdom. Key figurehead at the time: Prof Lain Martin

Jubilee Gospel Centre Bamenda. Key figure heads: Pastor Cletus Ndifor, Pastor Mbaku Gilbert and Pastor Philemon Bein.

Zion Baptist Church (ZBC) Cambridge. Key figure heads: Rev Gale Richards, Geoff Mann and Jane Mann.

By the way, this is not an exhaustive list of the incredible people and institutions that I am proud of in my life. I cannot include everyone on these few pages reserved for acknowledgements.

Notwithstanding, **a big THANK YOU** to you all. You have remarkably made me proud.

FOREWORD

I felt absolutely honoured when Joseph contacted me saying he would like me to write the foreword of his book. It is true I was aware of this project ever since its conception. But little did I know that it will hit me differently, of him finding me worthy of giving the opening statements to this ultra-modern and well-articulated piece.

Joseph is not a stranger to me. I knew him right back in the days of secondary school (at Sacred Heart College Douala) and I can say without any fear of contradiction that he has always proven his worth. You would find out exactly what I mean as you go through every single page of this book.

As a commercial and business student for many years and as one running multiple online businesses, I personally do appreciate the worth of what Joseph has compiled to form what makes the content of this book. Digitalization and e-commerce is absolutely the 'new normal' for startups and SMEs who are forward looking and wish to scale up their businesses to limitless levels.

As I went through the content of what is compiled by this brilliant mind, I could gather clearly that he wasn't against young entrepreneurs building other skills such as leadership skill, organizational skill, teamwork skill, communication skill etc., but he was just simply laying more emphasis on the importance of digital skills and how startups and SME's can leverage on it and see an undeniable transformation in their businesses.

Even whilst making emphasis on digitalization and e-commerce as the way to go, he wasn't blind to the challenges and difficulties that startups and SME owners especially in Africa (Cameroon in particular), do face on a day to day basis. This book is very real and practical.

Let me be careful not to expose everything about the book before time. I will let you give it a go so you can join me appreciate the effort he has put to get this piece together. Do sit back, relax and treat yourself with a great content that you need in order to take your startup and SME to the next level.

Nke Cynthia,
Online Business expert,
Digital Entrepreneur,
Germany.

Words to look out for as you read:

Simultaneously – At the same time

SME'S - Small and Medium Size Enterprises

'Backbone' employee- An indispensable key worker

Delineate – Describe precisely

Semantic exercise - Relating to meaning in language or logic

Imperative - Of vital importance

Leverage - Use to maximum advantage

Encompass - Surround and have or hold within

The cloud - A remote version of a data center which lets you access your data through the internet away from your company's physical premises.

Pivotal - Of crucial importance in relation to the success of something

SSL Certificate - Secure Socket Layer Certificate

Opportunists – Someone who takes advantage of opportunities immediately they arise whether having planned on them or not

Modus operandi – A particular way/method of doing something.

The west – The western part of the world such as Europe and North America

ECOWAS – Economic Community of West African States

EAC – Eastern African Community

SADC – Southern African Development Community

CEMAC – Economic and Monetary Community of Central Africa

COMESA – Common Market for Eastern and Southern Africa

SACU – Southern African Customs Union

TABLE OF CONTENTS

DEDICATION 1

ACKNOWLEDGEMENTS 3

FOREWORD... 7

INTRODUCTION.. 15

PURPOSE OF THIS BOOK 18

CHAPTER 1 20

1.0 THE 5 PRACTICAL REALITIES WHICH UNIQUELY LIMIT OWNERS OF STARTUPS AND SME'S IN CAMEROON IN TERMS OF DIGITALIZATION AND E-COMMERCE 20

CHAPTER 2 29

2.0 DEFINING TERMINOLOGIES: 29

2.1 DIGITIZATION.. 29

2.2 DIGITALIZATION: 32

2.3 E-COMMERCE.. 39

CHAPTER 3..**43**

A.

3.0 THE JOURNEY THROUGH TIME PAST: (JOYNER, 2020)..**43**

B.

3.1. E-COMMERCE STATISTICS..**48**

C.

3.2 TYPES OF E-COMMERCE BUSINESSES: **51**

CHAPTER 4..**58**

A.

4.0 THE AFRICAN CONTINENT IN LIGHT OF DIGITAL TRANSFORMATION AND E-COMMERCE IN INTERNATIONAL BUSINESS..**58**

B.

4.1. CAMEROON'S INVOLVEMENT IN E-COMMERCE AND DIGITAL INNOVATION **63**

CHAPTER 5..**67**

5.0 WHAT IS THE WAY FORWARD AND WHAT CAN BE DONE DIFFERENTLY TO TRY AND MEET UP WITH THE TIMES?................................... 67

CHAPTER 6...85

6.0 HIGHLY RECOMMENDED INNOVATION HUBS AND STARTUP INCUBATORS IN CAMEROON AND THE CONTINENT OF AFRICA............................ 85

CHAPTER 7...89

7.0 HOPE FOR THE FUTURE: 89

BIBLIOGRAPHY: 91

APPENDICES: 93

INTRODUCTION

The business world has witnessed all kinds of technological innovations in the last decade. It is quite fascinating how there are ongoing debates on whether we are still at the start of the digital age or perhaps already in a post-digital era. No matter where we are on the timeline of digital technology, one thing is sure; technology has come to stay.

> *"No matter where we are on the timeline of digital technology, one thing is sure; technology has come to stay".*

It doesn't come as a surprise to anyone that the year 2020 was predominantly marked by events surrounding the global pandemic. As the world attempts to simultaneously cope with and battle the invisible enemy; Covid-19, there seem to have emerged the frequent use of the phrase **"the new normal".**

This phrase is intended to mean; *a new way of tackling day-to-day life as opposed to the old ways prior to the diseases' outbreak*. Following the same line of thought, I also think it is not wrong to regard technological innovation as **'the new normal'** in the world of business.

If businesses (particularly startups and SME's) want to stay relevant and scale up to national and international levels, they inevitably would need to look for ways to incorporate digital technology to their scope of operation. They would also module themselves differently from how they operated before.

Due to the grave nature of the pandemic, many organizations in the United Kingdom and other parts of the world laid off their workers. Many workflows were then digitized as employees were required to work remotely from home.

Online stores such as **amazon, eBay** and **Shopify** witnessed a boom in their operations and earnings. They were smart to have caught the vision of the **'new normal'** early enough and were already operating within it. Irrefutable changes in the business world have happened within very short notice in the last decade, let alone, the start of 2020. It then goes without saying that moving forward, **digitization, digitalization and**

e-commerce are the core recipes for International business as per the title of this book.

I am by no means saying this is an exhaustive list of elements to consider in an attempt to scaling up to national and international levels in business. I am simply saying that, *major paradigm shifts in today's business world is geared towards digitization, digitalization and e-commerce*. This is in cognizance of disruptions which have happened in the last decade especially the most recent pandemic of 2020.

PURPOSE OF THIS BOOK

The essence of this book is not to scare individuals or businesses operating on either local, national or global scales. It is, however, meant to draw our attention to the fact that; *certain changes in global business outlook have occurred so fast and these changes have definitely come to stay.* In effect, **there undoubtedly needs to be an accompanying paradigm shift in our normal business modules, routines and operations if we need to live up with the times**.

Large Multinational corporations are no exception to this. **Nonetheless, startups and SME's need to be keener on digitization and online presence if they wish to scale up their operations to national and international levels.**

"To lay bare the fact that: Digitalization and E-Commerce are crucial for Startups and SME's in the continent of Africa willing to live up with the times and scale up to national and International levels in business"

18

This book would borrow plenty of events and examples within Europe, America and Africa. However, *a wakeup-call will mostly be directed towards start-ups and SMEs in the continent of Africa which are neither showing interest in going digital yet nor are proving active in augmenting their existing digital skills*.

I spent 22years of my life in Cameroon, a country which is located in West and Central Africa before was later exposed to alternative digital experiences in other parts of the world. I thought of warning you ahead just because some of the stories I will share in this book are massively shaped by where I have spent my life the most.

Let's get straight into it.

I begin by exposing some realities in Cameroon as to where Start-ups and SME's are at, with regards to digitization and e-commerce. This would serve as a starting point to **the practical realities** and **theoretical knowledge** this book intends to pass across.

CHAPTER 1

1.0 The 5 Practical Realities which uniquely limit owners of Startups and SME's in Cameroon in terms of Digitalization and E-Commerce

Before delving into these practical realities, I must emphasize on the fact that I deliberately used WhatsApp instead of email communication to collect the data I needed on this topic of interest (Digitization, Digitalization and E-Commerce). I communicated over **120 Cameroonians** who either run a startup, or work for an SME in Cameroon.

WhatsApp communication creates a down-to-earth atmosphere of relaxation among respondents. There is less consciousness about professionalism on WhatsApp when matched with Email communication. This enabled me to get the kind of honest and sincere practical realities I was trying to gather from respondents. These limiting realities for Start-ups and SMEs in Cameroon are discussed below:

''Hey Jo'o please let me call you back later. My data is low, I have low battery and electricity has been cut''.

I forwarded the research survey to a lady running a small hair salon in the city of **Bamenda**. I asked her if she has integrated any digital aspects into her business and if she would like to share with me. This was her immediate reply "

1. *"Hey Jo, Please let me call you back later. My data is low, I have low battery and electricity has been cut".*

Little did she know that she was already revealing some of the **practical realities I was looking for**; No light (electricity), limited mobile data, and probably low quality of the device (telephone) she has.

"I could decipher the reality of: limited electricity supply, limited mobile data and possibly low quality of the device (mobile phone) she has".

These were major practical concerns I could already decipher from her reply before she ever got back to me again with her 'real' answers. I wouldn't have gotten this sincere truth from her if I had used email as the means of communication.

2. *"I have neither a website nor email address. Many of my clients come through referrals from those I have served before".*

I received a fairly large number of replies with over **78%** of **120 respondents** not having websites for their small businesses. An employee of a small Graphic Design Enterprise in Douala said they had neither a website nor any social media page for their business. You might be quick to think that their graphic design skills meant they had more digital options for their customers but they didn't.

"Displaying goods/services via WhatsApp statuses tends to be a prominent way for many small business owners in Cameroon to engage with their customers/ potential customers".

The few having online presence mentioned a business page on Facebook, but do not seem to be engaging with it often. They rather prefer displaying samples of their products/services via WhatsApp statuses. This sounded like their favourite way of engaging with their online community.

3. *"The thoughts of switching from paper based to computer based operation is quite expensive as this will imply the need for computer, internet connection, data servers and security"*

A key staff of a Digital Innovation Organization in the capital city of Yaoundé said the above statement is what he frequently hears clients say when trying to sell his digital products and services to them.

"Increased service cost, fear of being scammed and lack of technical know-how"

From his assessments, other triggers to this statement are; clients fear being scammed online, increased service cost and the lack of technical knowhow.

4. *'I haven't thought of innovating my business because what I do is just part-time whilst going to school. When I complete my studies I will look for a proper job"*

As I got this reply, I could immediately spot a mindset problem. The inclination towards a regular job after studies sometimes deters talented youths from exploring their

"The inclination towards a regular job after studies sometimes deters talented youths from exploring their entrepreneurial potentials even whilst on their academic courses"

entrepreneurial and innovative potentials whilst on their academic courses in school. This is a real limiting problem.

This statement quickly reminds me of **Robert Kiyosaki's** opinion on education systems in his bestselling book **"Rich Dad, Poor Dad"**. Most education systems in the world were designed during the industrial era. The school systems prepared graduates and elites to get white Collar, blue collar and pink collar jobs in cognizance of their usefulness in the factories.

Many economies in the world including Cameroon have not redesigned their education system to well suit the current information age. **Philemon Bein (2020),** in his book; **'Financial Education; The missing education in our school system'** also insisted that, in as much as school education is important, Financial education is key to those willing to get ahead and live prosperous lives and careers.

This start-up owner would not bother augmenting digital aspects to her business, let alone, innovating it in any other way because she wants to be reliant on her regular job upon graduation.

5. *"I don't like to post my business on social media. It's just as if am showing off or begging people to buy from me"*

This statement tells a lot about how our mindsets can be a huge deterrent to our success in business; whether large or small. Many startup and SME owners in Cameroon are account holders of at least two of the following social media networks: **Facebook, Instagram, Snapchat, YouTube, Twitter, LinkedIn** and in recent times; **TikTok** etc.

Notwithstanding, many of them have not yet come to the knowledge of how vital these platforms can be for their business success. Examples; **using these platforms to reaching wider audiences, getting feedback for services rendered, advertising, sales** and the list goes on.

"There is a way commercial posts can be made with professionalism and integrity across so many social media platforms"

There actually could be some legitimate reasons why small business owners might choose NOT to take their business on social media depending on who is involved and what is at stake.

However, some others don't just fancy leveraging the use of social media to grow and expand their businesses. **They perhaps**

interpret it as 'showing off' or 'begging people to buy'. This mindset is not the right one for business in today's digital age.

There is a way commercial posts can be made with professionalism and integrity across so many social media platforms. This is a very vital skill that people with the above mentality should learn and practice should they desire to grow their small businesses.

There are loads and loads of practical realities to share as I gathered from respondents in different parts of Cameroon. It is just not possible to include everything in this book.

It was very essential to have teased out the day-to-day practical but limiting realities for small businesses in Cameroon. This helps in disclosing where we are now and to envisage where we wish to be in light of digitization and e-commerce.

Now, let us get a bit academic and educate ourselves on:

> ➢ What Digitization, Digitalization and E-commerce really mean.

> ➢ Of what relevance are they to start-ups and SME's

> ➢ What can be done to promote and sustain them in Cameroon and the entire Continent of Africa?

CHAPTER 2

2.0 Defining terminologies: Digitization, Digitalization and E-commerce.

2.1 Digitization

Many traditional businesses have always highly depended on key individuals in an enterprise. These key individuals are sometimes regarded as the **'backbone'** of some or all of the business' day-to-day operations. This 'backbone' phenomenon still holds true even

"Digitization in its simplest form is the conversion of analogue information to digital or electronic format"

for modern businesses today. However, with the emergence of digitization, the very relevant skills and knowledge that those indispensable individuals or groups may possess can now be digitally converted into data, processed, stored and can be retrieved even in their absence.

This goes a long way in making modern businesses coping to a greater extent even without the so called 'backbones' or indispensables. **The business dictionary** defines **Digitization** as *the conversion of analogue information to digital/electronic format with suitable electronic devices so that information can be processed, stored and transmitted through digital circuits, equipments and networks.*

Digitization graphic 2.1.1

As an indigene of the African Continent particularly from Cameroon, I successfully completed an online application to study abroad without having unnecessary back-and-forth conversations with the admissions officers. This was because all the academic and international information they required of me at the initial stages of my application were all in digital format and available online.

They also ensured that this information (online application form) could possibly be accessed by potential candidates (such as myself) via an electronic device (phone/laptop) on their website. This is digitization.

Let me cite another example; the global pandemic in 2020 forced managements of organizations to implement remote working for their employees due to enforced lockdown. Organizations had to revisit their knowledge management system to ensure that relevant data and documents were all in one central location. This was to allow for easy access by every employee who needed them from home via remote workspace. This is digitization.

It is said that when Knowledge management system is built to allow for collaboration between teams, that is a digital workplace enabled.

Worthy of note is the fact that, the term **Digitization** lays much emphasis just on the **information conversion** to electronic format. Hence, when **the entire benefits of the digitization processes** are considered, it perhaps leads us to the term; **Digitalization**.

2.2 Digitalization:

I am sure by now smart thinkers are starting to **delineate** the difference in these two terms as they read further. These terms are often confusing to users and widely used interchangeably in the world of information technology. Nonetheless, we shall attempt to try and bring about clarity in their distinction.

It is termed **Digitalization** *when organizations leverage their digital processes to improve and enhance overall business operations.* This definition further explains what we earlier mentioned above -*'the benefits of the digitization processes'.*

If further down the line, we are also keen on the benefits of **Digitalization processes**, it then perhaps leads us to **Digital Transformation.**

> *"Digitalization is when organizations leverage their digital processes to improve and enhance overall business operations"*

This is not meant to be a **semantic exercise.** Even prominent authors themselves on modern innovation and extreme digital transformation have not bothered a lot in emphasizing the distinctiveness of these terminologies. However, since this book perhaps emphasizes **digitization and digitalization** as the 'new normal' for Startups and SME's in dire need of achieving local, national and international expansion, it is imperative therefore, that the distinction of these terminologies is made known and clear.

That said.

Let us now take a look at an example that encompasses the meaning of **Digitization, Digitalization, and Digital Transformation:**

*Mr. Adam runs a real estate firm and manages a property which he lets out to tenants. If Mr. Adam scans and saves the tenancy agreement as a PDF copy in his drive C of his office computer, then that is **Digitization**.*

*Now, if Mr. Adam goes further and saves the PDF copy of the tenancy agreement to **'the cloud'** so he can remotely access it from anywhere and at any time, then that is **Digitalization**. This is because, the digitization process has been leveraged to improve his business operations irrespective of his present location.*

Following the above example, it is safe to say **digitization** is a sure means to achieving **digitalization** and not the other way round.

Let us also clarify ourselves on another frequently used terminology; **Digital Transformation.** This terminology, put in simple terms means *'the combined benefits of digitalization'.* **David Burkett (2017)** suggests a very contemporary example of digital transformation in the advertising industry. **David** compares <u>traditional advertising via paper mail</u> versus <u>the modern approach to advertising via email</u>.

The Digital Transformation in his comparison is evident as modern marketers are now able to know exactly <u>how many potential customers received and opened emails sent to them, the pieces of content they chose to engage with</u> <u>and the potentials the customers are exhibiting</u>. These benefits were clearly not achievable back in the days of paper advertising.

Modern digital marketers now have all the data they need to make an accurate calculation and prediction of what is or isn't working in the field. This then helps them to customize a more accurate target marketing content to potential customers. This is **Digital Transformation** which comes about as a result of *combined positive effects of Digitalization*. This is the 'new normal' for businesses (both large and small) that are forward looking to a wider scope of operation.

Digital transformation graphic 2.2.1

Digital technology has so much to offer businesses. But statistically speaking (which we will get into later), a major part of the African continent is not benefiting from it as much as it should. The continent is simply not prepared.

Let me share another experience. Permit me stick to the aspect of online application forms once again. I will be referring to the education sector of Cameroon this time.

I am one of the privileged Cameroonians who attended the best schools available in the country. By this, I refer to Primary, secondary, high school and the university. I can confirm that I have never, in Cameroon, filled in an online application form for admission into an educational institution. Instead, you need to go on campus, queue up to collect the paper forms, fill them in and submit in an office.

If part of the process is for you to make a one-time application fee deposit with your form, you then need to go queue up again in the banks till whatever time they attend to you. Sadly, there were simply no online options for all these hassles.

Apart from the education sector, the transport sector didn't seem to be any different. I have never purchased a travel ticket online to travel across towns in the country.

The online options for these services were just not available. As

I write, my researches do not indicate any significant changes from the experiences I just shared.

The essence of these shared experiences is neither to ridicule my home country nor to undermine my previous institutions (alma maters). I still identify with them today with so much prestige and nobility.

The intention is to be practical and sincere about how little we (Cameroonians) are benefitting from digitization on our day to day lives compared to other parts of Africa and the wider world.

Owners of these institutions might think they are doing fine by managing their processes the way they are currently doing. But until they get to that point of desiring the benefits of digitalization, they might never understand what they are missing out on.

Let's be clear; I am not ignorant of the fact that operating on a high digital scale would need quite a lot to be in place – both **internally** within the organization and **externally** within the business environment

I am also not ignorant of the fact that businesses are out to serve the needs of customers and should tailor their activities to be more customer-centric. Sadly, this sometimes happen even to the detriment of the organizations' innovation plans.

Further down the line, we will be discussing why many startups and SME's find it very challenging to go digital. Just remain curious as you read on.

The survey for data collection which was sent around to gather first-hand information from startups and SME owners in Cameroon, will be added at the end of this book as an appendix.

2.3 E-Commerce

It is no news that the emergence of the internet has brought about an immeasurable transformation in the business world. There are clearly still individuals and businesses who might not have conducted transactions over the internet due to poor internet connection or no internet access in their area.

However, many individuals and businesses both in the developing and the developed world are benefiting from purchases and sales conducted electronically via the use of the internet. This is simply <u>electronic commerce</u> or <u>e-commerce</u>.

Ecommerce graphic 2.3.1

Recent statistics have proven beyond reasonable doubts that e-commerce has gained so much grounds in recent years. *It is impossible for businesses (both large and small) to stay relevant and globally competitive if they do not integrate the internet into major components of their business transactions.*

Before we get into the e-commerce **statistics** and the existing **e-commerce types and platforms**, let us briefly **retrace the past** and remind ourselves of previous commercial developments which unfolded before today's digital era.

CHAPTER 3

A.

3.0 The journey through time past: (Joyner, 2020)

One of the world's leading digital marketing expert; **Mark Joyner** in his book **"Your Roadmap to Money in 2020"** expatiated on some of the commercial routes the world has witnessed right up until where we are today.

- **In the 1700's**, there was already the emergence of general stores as pioneer owners were committed to serving the local needs of the small towns in which they were. Here, Pioneer business owners often sold to consumers directly.

-The rise of the industrial revolution **in 1760** saw mass production.

The industrial revolution was a period of time which recorded a transition where the production of goods moved from households and small shops to factories. This period lasted for over 100years. It kick-started in Great Britain and then later spread throughout Europe and then America.

The industrial Revolution witnessed two phases (Late 1700's to mid-1800 and mid-1800 to early 1900 respectively): **First Industrial Revolution** (where steam engine and cotton gin played significant roles) and **the Second Industrial Revolution** (where more technology was used to mass produce goods). More technological innovation was due to the presence of electricity, production line and the Bessemer Steel Process. Since this phase saw mass production in factories, producers then found the need to **uniquely identify their brands as the only way to be visible.**

<u>**-In 1859**, the first Chain Store was opened in Memphis Tennessee, USA</u>.

Chain stores started emerging because of both mass production and branding combined. Departmental Stores, Grocery Stores, General/Variety Stores and Specialty shops gained grounds in order to adapt to the modern trend at the time.

Producers of goods needed their brands to always be readily available in the chain stores for the sake of consistency in products sold. This limited the chances of customers switching to alternatives amidst the mass production.

It should be noted that it was around this same era that USA witnessed the **"gold rush"** in California which turned out to be another big news at the time. This took place around **mid to late 1800's**. Many **opportunists** at the time saw it as another great way to stay on top of the game. Yet, it rather turned out that those who got rich in the gold rush was not necessarily the miners themselves but the merchants selling the shovels and pick axes the miners needed.

Worthy of note here is the fact that that **Levi's** became one of the trusted clothing brands that benefited from this rush. The miners could rely on them to get the sort of rugged jeans they needed for the rush in California.

Business owners started reaping the benefits of big and multiple chain stores, so they thought of making it even bigger in the name of Superstores.

This made it even more difficult for smaller stores to survive. **Mark** described the situation as; *"the superstores sucking out all the oxygen in the room for smaller businesses"*. Small competitors clearly could not survive and had to seek for jobs from the giant Superstores. They became economically unviable to stay operational.

Superstores are broadly categorized into **Mega Specialty Chains, Departmental Stores, Supermarkets and Hypermarkets.**

Research suggests that the internet was first introduced in the **1960's** and was intended for military purposes.

The internet technology then started evolving until it saw the first ecommerce transaction in **August 1994**. The transaction was made by **Phil Brandenberger of Philadelphia who used his MasterCard to purchase 'Sting's Ten Summoners' over the internet for $12.48.**

This transaction was so **pivotal** and served as a wakeup-call to the world that the internet could be a great place for commercial transactions. The internet then officially became a safe ground to buy and sell products/services in **1995** with the issuing of the **SSL Certificate**. A safe encryption technology was now available via a **Secure Socket Layer (SSL)** to enhance safe purchases over the internet. This was how Electronic Commerce was officially born.

B.

3.1. E-Commerce Statistics

Hard facts and data have always been very far-reaching with regards to understanding any particular commercial sector. We shall pull relevant e-commerce statistics from the following sources: **99Firms** *(E-commerce Statistics for 2020)*, **Finance Online** *(2020 Data and Market Share Analysis)* and **Statista** *(E-commerce share of total retail sales from 2015 to 2023).*

The above web and software development organizations frequently publish the latest e-commerce statistics which can be quite helpful for entrepreneurs willing to explore their online options. Still, it could be quite helpful just to know how well the sector is performing. Consider the statistics below:

❖ There are predictions that retail e-commerce sales can hit $4.13 trillion at the end of 2020.

❖ Predictions of 95% of all purchases to be via e-commerce by 2040.

❖ The possibility of a 24/7 purchase time makes e-commerce even more attractive as customer transactions are not restrained by time.

❖ About 51% of digital buyers use their smartphones to do so.

❖ Free Shipping to customers is a huge factor influencing their chance of shopping online.

❖ Around 93% of the purchasing decisions of online shoppers are greatly influenced by the visual appearance of the online store and the items displayed.

❖ Facebook registers up to 80% of all social media purchases.

❖ Predictions of mobile e-commerce retail sales reaching 3.5 trillion by 2021.

❖ Credit Card was the preferred means of payment for up to 42% online shoppers in 2017.

❖ Online stores with active social media presence has 32% more sales.

❖ Online reviews have accounted for over 55% of all online shopping

❖ China's e-commerce market is the world's fastest growing one with an estimated e-commerce value of 672 billion in 2017.

❖ Google Searches account for over 43% of all e-commerce traffic

C.
3.2 Types of E-Commerce Businesses:

It is not enough to think of e-commerce just as buying and selling over the internet. The type of e-commerce transaction completed is further categorized in terms of:

1. **the parties involved in the transaction,**
2. **the goods or services sold**
3. **the operating platform used**

When categorized **according to the partied involved, we can pinpoint 7 basic models** of this type of e-commerce transactions with completely different purchasing dynamics.

I. **Business to Business (B2B)**

Examples: An independent auditing firm offering auditing services to a micro-finance institution. Also, the type of business relationship existing between the manufacturer of a product and a wholesaler. These are Business to Business transactions, hence B2B.

II. Business to Consumer (B2C)

Examples: Making a purchase on amazon, eBay, Jumia or Etsy etc. Also, making a click-and-collect transaction in-store is a B2C transaction. Shops well known for click and collect in the UK include Argos, John Lewis, Marks and Spencer, Boots and NEXT.

It should be noted that **the above two (B2B and B2C) are the main models of e-commerce transactions** based on the parties involved. That said. Let us get a bit more critical to discover some few more as listed below:

III.   Consumer to Consumer (C2C)

Examples: Buying and selling on a social media platform like Facebook.

PayPal is well known for being a frequently used payment option to such transactions. Another example for a C2C transaction is through platforms such as eBay or Craigslist.

IV. Consumer to Business (C2B)

Examples: Getting a satisfied customer to write a review on your business website for a discount. Also, by organizing a referral program. Here, a referral bonus is promised an existing customer who refers other potential customers to the business

V. Business to Government (B2G)

Some people also refer to this type as **Business to Administration (B2A)**. Examples: An agreement which permits a private research institute to conduct research which the government uses to influence decisions of a city. Also, an independent body to organize, manage and supervise the political election program of a country. In Cameroon, this is supposed to be the role of **ELECAM**; Elections Cameroon (in English), ELECTION CAMEROUNAISE (in French).

VI. Consumer to Government (C2G)

Some people also refer to this type as **Consumer to Administration (C2A)**. Examples: Individuals paying income tax to the government which is deducted from source. Also, paying for health insurance, utility bills, visa fees etc., means you are engaging in a C2G transaction.

VII. Government to Business (G2B)

Examples: The government subsidizing the cost of establishing a computer lab in a private school. Also, a government agency offering e-learning facility to a private institution. That is a G2B transaction.

When e-commerce is categorized according to the products and services typically sold online, we can pinpoint three types as below:

I. **Stores typical of physical goods:**

Examples of such e-commerce stores include **Zapppos;** an online shoe retailer. **Bonobos** an online store for menswear. Customers may want it delivered to them or may choose to click-and-collect instore.

II. Stores typical of offerings services:

Examples include online consultation services and also, the

services of an online educator. Service based e-tailers as such often want customers to pre-book appointments prior to service delivery. This allows for the possibility of the service to be well tailored to suit the specific needs of the customer.

III.   Stores typical of offering digital products;

Examples: **coursera** (an online platform for online learning). **Audiobooks** (a website where audiobooks can be bought and sold). Other examples are software, graphics and virtual goods.

When classifying e-commerce according to the platform used, we are referring to the established software applications that allows online businesses to manage their website, market their products or services, conduct sales and fulfilment operations. Examples of such platforms include:

Amazon, eBay, Alibaba, Shopify, Etsy, Fiverr, Upwork, Jumia, WooComerce, BigCommerce, Volusion, Drupal Commerce, Oracle Commerce, SalesForce, etc.

Many other useful details with regards to the pros, cons, distinctiveness and individual statistics of each of these platforms can be investigated further on **ecommerceguide.com.**

Now, let's just pause and make some reflections

We have spent quite some time trying to define terminologies, journeying through time and learning from the past. We have looked at available statistics and have also broken down the different types of ecommerce categories.

Now, what?

The essence of all these was **to have a real background knowledge of digitization and e-commerce so as to get to that point of accepting them as the new reality in today's business world.**

Again, it will be practically impossible for start-ups and SME's to scale up from local to national and international levels without integrating digital technology to their **modus operandi.**

Let us not forget the initial thoughts we held at the start of this book:

➢ Where about is the African continent in all these? That is; Digital Transformation and E-commerce in International Business?

➢ How involved is Cameroon with Digital Technology in Business?

CHAPTER 4

A.

4.0 The African continent in light of digital transformation and e-commerce in International Business

Isn't it surprising today that when referring to international business, it quickly translates in the minds of some Africans as *'closing a business deal with a European, American or Chinese'*? This kind of mentality must be ditched.

The standard for going international must not necessarily mean a scenario where one is on business talks with Americans, Europeans or Chinese or the west in general. I say this because the African regions are at the threshold of seeking to build a solid business partnership within themselves as a continent.

This partnerships should be prioritized by Africa's political and economic leaders to reinforce the continents economic strength.

Working out an agreement on the pan-continental free trade zones of the <u>six trade blocks in Africa</u> is key for Africa's economic stability and International business endeavors. Trade blocks here include CEMAC, ECOWAS, SADC, COMESA, EAC and SACU.

That said; whether the international business transactions are taking place among Africans within the African regions itself or intercontinentally with Eurasia, Australia or the Americas, it is imperative to know and understand that digital transformation and e-commerce will play a crucial part. This is the new-normal for businesses seeking a globally competitive edge.

The continent of Africa is very large in size and population, second only to the Asian Continent. **The internet world Stats** predicted Africa's population for 2020 as over 1.3 billion. Out of this number, over 526 million were internet users in 2019 making a penetration rate of about 39.3%.

Isn't it obvious that the African continent is going through a phase of digital transformation even though not at a pace that it ought? The continent of Africa has a big appetite for e-commerce.

Sacha Poignonnec, the Cofounder and co-CEO of **Jumia** confirmed Africa's appetite for e-commerce in a video documentary published by **Mackinsey and Company** on the 17th of January 2019. **Sacha** was quite amazed at how the African online market bought up to 10 mobile phones on the first day of operation when Jumia was launched. Nobody knew about Jumia by then but they started recording success on their first day of operation. This is just confirming Africa's huge appetite for e-commerce.

The CEO and his team felt impressed as customers from the African online market didn't go only for the cheap stuff online. They sometimes went for the expensive products too. A very promising aspect of e-commerce in Africa is its population. That is; over 1.3 billion people. So many of them are very connected and we have just seen above how the internet penetration rate is growing too; 39.3% in 2019.

E-commerce has brought about a shift in the operating pattern for many startups in Africa. For example: It is now quite possible to begin an online business with little capital, nurture it to see it grow and then could later consider opening a physical store in addition to the online presence. The reverse holds true as to how many would have loved to do it from the traditional perspective. That is; having an offline store first before taking it online.

Reports by **Statista** reveal that total e-commerce transactions in 2017 was valued at $16.5 billion with predictions of this figure rising to $75 billion by 2025. The African continent must not relent her efforts to benefit from this promising global e-commerce market exhibiting huge potentials.

On the other hand, there are some reasons why e-commerce isn't growing in the African continent as much as it ought. **Nicolas Goldstein;** *the cofounder of Talenteum Africa,* holds the opinion that, it is extremely hard to make predications which are *'close to accurate'* anticipation of e-commerce value for Africa. **Nicola** opines based on the work load that needs to be done on the African online landscape to ensure a safe and more accurate value predictions. If not, the predicted values will just be a complete waste of time as they might be very far from reality.

UNCTAD made a global ranking of the growing concerns surrounding the e-commerce landscape in Africa. **UNCTAD** stands for the *United Nations Conference on Trade and Development*. The ranking was based on **the average of four main indicators**, namely:

o <u>The proportion of the population with access to the internet</u>
o <u>The proportion of the population with access to a bank account</u>
o <u>The level of security of the web-servers</u>
o <u>The reliability of the postal services.</u>

Reports reveal that African countries were ranked **'low' (below average)** when matched with the value of the above indicators and index of each country. As **Talenteum Africa** reveals, **Mauritius, Nigeria and South Africa** which were the best scoring African countries were still found at the bottom of the ranking. The truth is, being lowly ranked does not give Africa a competitive edge on the face of global business. In this regard, Africa needs to sit up and reconstruct their digital space and also revisit their enabling environment for real e-commerce business to take place.

B.

4.1. Cameroon's involvement in e-commerce and Digital Innovation

Cameroon, which is often termed *'Africa in Miniature'* is classed as one of the most urban nations of Africa. This goes a long way to explain the significant internet penetration rate in the country making her top three in Africa with regards to internet access.

The Bank of Scotland published reports in July 2020, disclosing that the number of internet users in Cameroon more than doubled over the last five years. The higher the internet users, the higher the chances of electronic commerce to take place. The internet is a prerequisite for e-commerce transactions. Good news is; Cameroon is aware of this and is working hard to step up her game.

Research suggests that; the most recent statistics for internet access in Cameroon was officially published in 2017. The official population of Cameroon at the time (2017) was over 25.5million people. 23% were connected to the internet, 16.9% of households owned a computer and 21.7% had internet access at home. Mobile broadband subscription was 17.7 per 100 inhabitants.

As a result of the Anglophone crises in the country, there were frequent internet cuts particularly in the English speaking regions as they stood up against marginalization from an oppressive French speaking regime.

It is but obvious that if 2020 statistics were released today, these numbers will even be more positive and would go a long way to further confirm the level of exponential growth of e-commerce in Cameroon.

It is also quite obvious that e-commerce in Cameroon is not growing at the pace at which it ought. **Kenya, Ghana and Nigeria** are quite ahead of Cameroon in the e-commerce sector. This does not, nonetheless, change the fact that the efforts made to leverage the e-commerce sector in Cameroon are moving towards the right direction.

As the number of internet users more than doubled in the last five years, the e-commerce market in Cameroon has grown to nearly ten folds over the last three years. This is amazing news isn't it?

The growth of e-commerce in Cameroon within the last few years wasn't achieved without some notable challenges. Cameroon is no exception to the four main indicators published by UNCTAD as seen earlier. However, the two most prominent challenges for Cameroon's e-commerce landscape are about **payment methods and logistics (address system for delivery).**

Payment methods tend to be a major challenge for e-commerce in Cameroon because Cameroon has limited local retail banking facilities. This perhaps hinders small business in Cameroon from expanding trade beyond national borders. Still in connection with payments, Cameroon has low penetration of bank cards which limits the Potentials for online purchases.

Majority of the population aren't quite sure about: *the associated cost of an online payment, the security involved in the payment traction, trust and accessibility* etc. These are all massive challenges around payments surrounding the e-commerce landscape of Cameroon.

It should be noted that some telecommunication network companies like **MTN, Orange and Nexxtel** are operating cheap mobile payment services which are much more affordable by both startups and existing SME owners. Mobile Payment Services here include: **MTN Mobile Money transfer, Orange Money transfer and Possa, respectively.**

The second major challenge to e-commerce in Cameroon is **logistics associated with the address system.** There is no fixed/definite address system in Cameroon which tends to thwart the delivery process. Destinations often lack street names and numbers. In this regard, customers have to be very specific in the description of where you can find them. E.g. *'the two story building block behind the garage opposite the roundabout'*

I can relate with this truth first-hand especially when I used to take a bike back home from school or the market. This is what I tell the bike man. *"Please take me above the hill next to **Ni John Fru Ndi's House**. At the end of the hill, turn left and keep going straight until the end of the road. The house with the green double doors is ours. Please drop me in front of it when we get there".*

The address and postal system in Cameroon is a disaster. For ecommerce to thrive, the address system obviously needs revisiting.

CHAPTER 5

5.0 What Is the Way Forward and What Can Be Done Differently to Try and Meet Up With The Times?

1. <u>**Do not minimize the small beginnings; Remain accountable to your business.**</u>

Even before trying to see reasons to take your business digital, it is of utmost importance to be very focused, intentional and committed with it. There is a single word which can describe what am heading towards. The word is **'accountability'.** If a business owner fails to be accountable, let him be accountable for his failure. The business can be small, yes, but do not minimize its potentials.

> *"If a business owner fails to be accountable, let him be accountable for his failure"*

It is true that it can be quite challenging for startups to begin operation in most African countries. For example; Cameroon. Nonetheless, can we pinpoint people who did a similar business in the same environment/conditions and managed to survive it? Of course, we can.

Philemon Bein (2020) exposed **'the Pitfalls that ruins financial ambitions'** in his recently published book titled: *Financial Education; the missing education in our school system.* One of the pitfalls was; **the edge to pursuing expensive brands in the market.** This pitfall is very critical as to why many small business owners become irresponsible with their businesses. Hence, their businesses tend to fail.

I am a young person and can absolutely relate to this pitfall. Oftentimes, we want to show up among our peers like a **fashionista** even when we don't have enough money to sustain the lifestyle. This makes our businesses to suffer.

A small business owner who is accountable for his business knows that any money taken out of the business is on **'borrow'** and he/she will do all to repay it back. Repaying it back is a sign of <u>responsibility</u> and <u>accountability</u>. This is one way a business can be sustainable and eventually grow.

Taking a sustainable business digital perhaps increases its chances of success. The reverse holds true for irresponsible business owners.

2. <u>Leveraging on social media presence to expand your business</u>

Arrey Bate (2019) was categorically clear in his book *(How to Make Money, Build Right Relationships with Social Media: Facebook and WhatsApp)* by laying bare that **'social media levels the playing field between brands'**. You just cannot estimate how many audiences you can

"You just cannot estimate how many audiences you can reach with your single post on social media"

reach with your single post on social media. With about 2years of working experience in the higher education sector in the United Kingdom, I understand the power of reaching out to students and potential students via social media communication in a highly professional context.

Facebook, Instagram, WhatsApp, Twitter, LinkedIn, YouTube, Reddit, TikTok etc., are all great social media platforms for business. NB; **Email** is a very great media platform too for business but isn't classed as a *'social media'* platform.

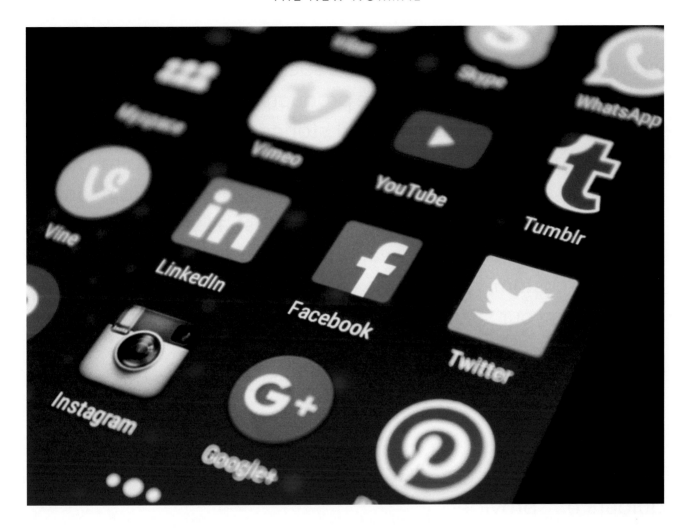

Social Media Graphic 5.2.1

Arrey insists that you can still make your social media mark very visible even in the presence of well established brands which existed long before yours.

Just decide today to leverage your social media presence. That is; create your business page on a social media platform such as Facebook, post and display the products/services professionally, share relatable and inspirational stories of your offerings from time to time, post clients feedback which can inspire others to choose your business over your competitors, join online communities with similar business interest as yours so you can learn from one another, love what you do and often engage with your customers. All these can go a long way within no time to enhance your sales and business growth.

3. <u>Receive mentorship from those who have gone ahead of us in the success we desire</u>

Mentorship is the guidance provided by a professional in a particular field. It goes a long way to put the mentee on track and ensures he/she does

"Even though a mentor can be available to provide professional guidance, a massive part of the business success still depends on the mentee implementing the professional advice"

NOT make possible startup mistakes the mentor made in his early days before growing to a competent professional.

Also, if your mentor is digitally inclined, he/she can identify aspects of your business that you can digitally explore.

Knowledge flow in mentorship is not only one way (from mentor to mentee). Sometimes, the mentors themselves are quite pleased and amazed with the brilliant ideas that mentees are bringing to the table.

Seeking a mentor is quite a sensible move for success in business and in life as a whole. Even though the mentor is available to provide guidance, a massive part of the business' success still depends on the mentee implementing the professional advice.

Mentorship graphic 5.3.1

Some higher education institutions in Cameroon partner with mentor organizations which from time to time offer mentorship to their students. If one is unlucky not to be part of such institutions, I highly recommend that it is worth sourcing for a mentor around you and paying for their services if that is the only way you can access them.

The value of mentorship to a mentee is far worth more than the cost of the mentorship program

I was also a victim of ignoring mentorship and professional advices for my business and academic career options in Cameroon. I only appreciated the value of mentorship when my university in the United Kingdom assigned one to me. The impact is so far-reaching. As I write, I still enjoy the guidance of my mentor.

4. **<u>Consider digital transformation an asset for your business and your desire to acquiring them might increase.</u>**

The answers I got from the survey proofed that many owners of startups and SME's tend to shy away from digitizing their businesses. Many of them do hold the following thoughts:

- **It requires increased capital**
- **It takes a lot of time to acquire the digital skills needed**
- **And lastly, many think the whole thing is just a complete waste of time.**

Yet, if we consider the benefits of digital transformation as an asset to our businesses instead of a liability, it will automatically eliminate most or all of the excuses above.

Some of the excuses may actually be legitimate as circumstances differ from person to person. Still, let us consider the old adage; *when there is a will, there is a way.*

If we consider digital skill as **asset** of which it is, then we will do all to it takes to acquire them.

5. <u>Familiarize yourself with advanced payment systems</u>;

E-commerce has grown so much so that those running online stores via **Amazon, eBay, Etsy,** or **Shopify** etc., can have huge and varied customers from different parts of the planet.

Clearly, stores which have multiple payment gateway options will have more

> *"Stores with multiple gateway payment options will have more competitive edge than those with limited payment gateway options"*

competitive edge. Examples of payment gateways include: **Visa Card, MasterCard, PayPal, Payeer, Skrill, WePay, Apple Pay, Google Checkout, Braintree, Cash App, E-Wallets** and so much more.

Payment-Gateway-Graphic 5.5.1

Familiarizing yourself with advanced global payment systems

is very important. There is no need losing a customer because you are limited by the kind of online payment options they use.

An online store or a small business must not necessarily have an account with absolutely all of what is listed above. That's not what I am trying to pass across. What I mean is; having enough payment options to suit your customers irrespective of their location on the globe, can make a big difference to the cash inflow of your business.

When your business has grown to a certain level, a partnership with **money transfer agencies** such as **Western Union, World Remit, MoneyGram, Small World, E-Teller** etc. could also make a huge difference for your business cash inflows.

6. **Operate your business with an open mind and know that there are customers at every level:**

There are customers for every business. Once a business has identified its niche market and is

"To intentionally capture the wealthy as customers, it would require you to operate at a level that you end up retaining them"

offering value, customers will always be available. The usual challenge for most startups and SME's is to retain and grow the customer base.

With that in mind, let's consider the financial sector in Cameroon as an example. The **Microfinance Institutions (MFI's)** in Cameroon targets <u>grass root customers</u> who struggle to access the services of the traditional banking system. Still in the same financial sector, there are **the commercial banks** whose mode of operations mostly capture <u>the middle class and high income earners</u> of the community. Again, there are **venture capitalists** who target <u>promising startups requiring more capital</u> to scale up and be successful.

The same analogy applies for startups and SME's in Cameroon. No matter which startup you have chosen, there are always customers available at any level if you offer value.

This is just to say it is good to have an open mind in business and not limit yourself to low thinking and low income earners. Meanwhile if you were realistically ambitious, you could target bigger/wealthier customers if you offered them real value.

Digital literacy and high standards of business operations usually tends out to be the norm for wealthy people. Therefore to intentionally capture the wealthy as customers, it would require you to operate at a level that you end up retaining them.

7. <u>Attend digital transformation seminars and innovation events around you</u>

There are two big benefits that are reaped from attending such seminars; **the skills you acquire** and **the network you build.** Just like I mentioned in the mentorship section earlier, the benefit you get from such programs in terms of *the skills acquired* and *network build* are

> *"The benefits you get from such programs in terms of skills acquired and network built are usually exponentially higher than the financial cost of the program"*

usually exponentially higher than the value of the cost of such programs.

So, consider such programs as <u>asset</u> to you and not liability.

8. <u>Build your e-commerce and digital skills using self-learning and development tools</u>

No doubt, we are in an information era. In as much as our formal regulated institutions of learning are very important in guiding us in our formation, self-learning is also very important as this is what allows for depth in our knowledge. It makes a huge difference.

"Self-Learning and Development is very important as it is what allows for depth in our knowledge"

There are quite a lot of useful videos and contents on YouTube and other social media platforms that can be used for self-learning and personal development.

There are very brilliant YouTube videos laying out the step by step guide on *how to setup an online store, how to make use of social media to grow your business or how to create an account with any of the renowned payment gateways such as PayPal, Cash App, E-wallets etc.,*

Once again, we are in an information age and google literally has almost all the answers or at least, very good suggestions of what we might be looking for. We can make positive use of these cheap and available information whilst being keen on the reliability of the information sources.

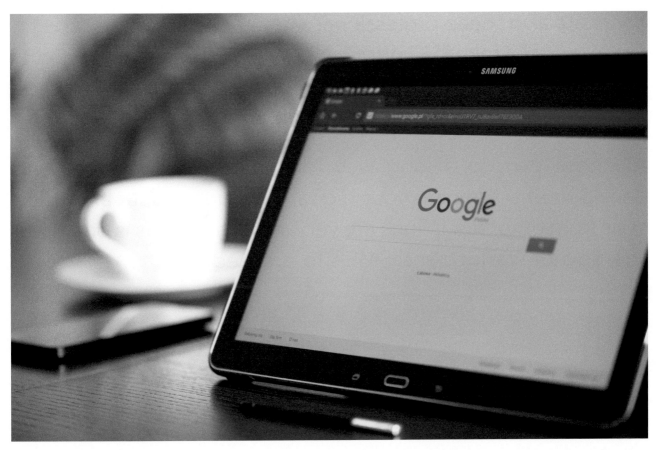

Internet-Search-Graphic 5.8.1

It is important to note that, not all information suggested by google is correct, valid or up-to-date. We need to use our good judgement and seek advice on the sources of information we are using to develop ourselves.

There are also cheap professional courses online to subscribe to. For example, **LinkedIn Learning** provides great video contents on aspects of all disciplines you desire. **Coursera** is also a renowned online education platform.

All these can go a long way to enhance self-learning and development. Keeping your digital skills up-to-date alongside skills from other disciplines are very important. This is one great strategy for startups and SME's to succeed.

CHAPTER 6

6.0 Highly recommended Innovation Hubs and Startup Incubators in Cameroon and the Continent of Africa

It was quite an honour to have a great insight on this subject matter from a Cameroonian veteran in the field. **Momo Bertrand** has substantially been part of multiple digital marketing projects in Africa and North America. He is currently the Digital Media Officer at ITCILO, a United Nations agency in Italy.

Gathering from **Bertrand's** responds following the research survey, there are quite some few innovation hubs and startup incubators in Cameroon that should be elevated to the view of young entrepreneurs looking forward to integrate digital skills to their businesses. Examples:

ACTIVSPACES brings together tech communities and further ensures that non-tech Savvy individuals and businesses benefit from digital innovative ideas.

ACMAR MEDIA GROUP is a huge independent integrated digital marketing agency serving the whole of West and Central Africa and still expanding its scope of operations.

OIC (Ocean Innovation Centres) provides a real digital economy platform for professionals, enthusiasts, developers, researchers and students.

TEKS GLOBAL AND VALUE CHAINS SERVICES; even though an agro-based investment company offering an ideal network marketing services, they are also keen on providing mentorship and support to promising innovative ideas for startups and SME's in Cameroon and beyond.

YALI (Young African Leader Initiative) of the former president of the United States of America; Barack Obama, aims to build young African leaders on diverse spheres on Africa. Digital innovation is no exception to their goals.

TONY ELUMELU FOUNDATION; a private African Foundation Championing Young Entrepreneurship across Africa.

VC4A is connecting Startup entrepreneurs with the knowledge, support programs, mentors and investors needed to succeed.

<u>CEI (Centre of Entrepreneurship and Innovation)</u> is an entrepreneurial practicing arm of CUIB (Catholic University Institute of Buea). This program is intended to facilitate innovation and help bridge the gap between theory and practice. Findings reveal that non-CUIB students can also fully participate with equal opportunities once their innovative business idea meets the required criteria.

It should be noted that programs such as <u>Tony Elumelu Foundation and YALI</u> are internationally recognized innovative programs. They go far beyond Cameroon and invites young innovative participants **across many parts of Africa**. The programs are quite intensive, highly competitive but also very exciting.

It is worth noting that this is obviously NOT an exhaustive list of effective innovation hubs and startup incubators in Cameroon.

CHAPTER 7

7.0 Hope for the Future:

From every indication, there is hope for startups and SME's in Cameroon and Africa to thrive via digital technology and the internet. There is so much untapped potentials in Africa which we collectively need to tap from. Ultimately, through <u>education</u>, <u>awareness programs,</u> and <u>practice</u>, we shall experience the paradigm shifts needed in today's business world to better equip ourselves for the new normal.

> *"There is so much untapped potentials in Africa which we collectively need to tap from"*

BIBLIOGRAPHY:

Alangeh, N. D., 2014. E-Commerce in Cameroon. *Denis&LenoraForetiaFoundation*, 1(1), pp. 1-19.

Arrey, A. B., 2019. *How To Make Money, Build Right Relationships With Social Media (Facebook & WhatsApp)*. 1 ed. Molyko-Buea: Bookman Publishers.

Bein, P., 2020. *Financial Education: The Missing Education In Our School System*. 1 ed. Buea: TEK MEDIA.

Bloomberg, J., 2018. Digitization, Digitalization And Digital Transformation: Confuse Them At Your Peril. *Forbes*, 1(1), pp. 1-9.

Burkett, D., 2020. How to Digitize Business Processes into Workflows. *Workingmouse*, 2(2), pp. 1-6.

Carmichael, C., 2020. Building Online Store. *WebsiteBuilderExpert*, 1(1), pp. 14-20.

Deslie, N., 2016. *Prospects and Challenges of Ecommerce in Cameroon*. [Online] Available at: https://www.academia.

edu/23163513/Prospects and challenges of Ecommerce in Cameroon [Accessed 5 August 2020].

Gibbins, E., 2017. 4 Ways Technology is Changing E-Commerce. *Numinix,* 1(1), pp. 1-3.

Goldstein, N., 2019. The Future of E-Commerce in Africa: A Mere Illusion?. *Business Opinion,* 1(1), pp. 1-3.

Jane, L. F., 2020. What is ecommerce in 2020? Ecommerce Definition Explained with examples. *ecommerce guide,* 6 July, 1(1), pp. 39-52.

Kiyosaki, R., 2018. *Rich Dad Poor Dad.* 5 ed. New York: Warner Books Ed.

Luenendonk, M., 2020. 27+ Genius Ways to Make Money Online Fast in 2020 (Earn Extra Income on the Side). *FounderJar,* 1(1), pp. 1-33.

Sable, D., 2012. A 'Post Digital' World, Really?. *ThinkWithGoogle,* 1(1), pp. 1-4.

APPENDICES:

Dear...................

I am pleased to get you involved in a little project I embarked on and would appreciate a *maximum of **30 Minutes** of your time*

I am currently writing a book on *Digitization, Digitalization and e-commerce in International Business* with the focus on Africa but even more specifically on Cameroon.

This is *NOT* meant for academic purposes as per se, but to help *sensitize and awaken the desire for most of the startups and SME's in Cameroon to think of ways to integrate and leverage the digital aspects of their businesses*

How would you be of help?

I chose you because I know you either own a small business in Cameroon or hold a senior level position in one.

Questions for the day.

1. Has your business been benefiting from digitalization?

Tip: the transition from a paper base (analogue) to electronic format may include:
*Creating a knowledge management system that can be accessed at anytime
*Building a website for your business, etc.

1. B. If yes, how and what digital aspects need improving? If no, why not?

2. Following the observations from your business, how are customers responding to digitalization in terms of payments: - Cash? Mobile money transfers? Bank transfer? Others?

3. Have the Internet and social media been significantly useful in anyways to promote your products /services? What platforms are your favourite to reach customers/potential customers?

Do you know of any Digital transformation Schemes or programs put in place by the government which can help improve the digital edge for your business?

Thank you for your time

End.

....

NB:

1. Your take on the above questions via *Voice note* on **WhatsApp** will be much appreciated.

2. You can also choose to ring me when you are able to do so. Tel: +44 7588139542, +44 7565294459

Lefor Joseph👤💼

Email: HYPERLINK "mailto:leforjoseph2@gmail.com"
leforjoseph2@gmail.com or HYPERLINK "mailto:lefor.
joseph@yahoo.com" lefor.joseph@yahoo.com
Facebook: Pappy Jo'o Lefor
Instagram: LeforJoseph
LinkedIn: Joseph Lefor
Snapchat: JO'O PAPPY
Twitter: Lefor Joseph